DAGPAW Means Success:
A Parent's Guide to Instilling Martial Arts Success Skills Into Their Child From Home

By
Rod Batiste
Former Full Contact Karate World Champion
Founder/Grand Master of WCRB Karate

© 2018 Rod Batiste, WCRB Karate
All Rights Reserved

1st Edition, Edited by Michael Hauck

ISBN-13: 978-0692057025 (WCRB Karate)
ISBN-10: 0692057021

The DAGPAW^{sm} curriculum is a service mark of WCRB Karate.

DAGPAW Means Success: A Parent's Guide to Instilling Martial Arts Success Skills Into Their Child From Home.

CONTENTS

Why I Wrote this Book 3
The Desire to Succeed 5
The Magic of DAGPAW 6
The Ugly Child Syndrome 8
What it Means to Succeed 12
Window of Success 14
The Age of Choices 17
Discipline: The D in DAGPAW 19
A's and B's: The First A in DAGPAW 29
Goal Setting: The G in DAGPAW 34
Perseverance: The P in DAGPAW 41
Attitude: The Second A in DAGPAW 46
Work Ethic: The W in DAGPAW 48
Teach DAGPAW Like a Master 50
Let's Get Started 52
What Parents Say about DAGPAW 53
APPENDIX A: Courtesy Champion Card. 56
APPENDIX B: To Do List 59
APPENDIX C Action Plan 60
APPENDIX D: About the Author 63
APPENDIX E: Martial Arts Studios Licensed to Teach
                The DAGPAW[sm] Curriculum 65

The DAGPAW^{sm} curriculum and the phrase "DAGPAW Means Success^{sm} are service marks of WCRB Karate.

Why I Wrote this Book

I grew up the second out of three children in a fatherless household. We were so poor that I can recall times when the whole family shared one egg for dinner.

For me, school was the most important institution in my life at the time – not for the education I was getting – but for the free food we got at breakfast and lunch.

My mother, who loved us and provided as well as she could, suffered with periodic bouts of bipolar schizophrenia and was afraid to stay in the house by herself. On welfare and unable to maintain a job because of her illness, she kept one of us at home with her every day because of her psychosis.

Growing up with one third of an education and a growing resentment with the bantering I got from kids in school when I was allowed to go, it didn't take me long to realize that I was doomed to failure.

Mom wanted the best for us and periodically told us so, but because of her condition, the situation we were in, and not knowing or associating with anyone who had made it, she didn't know how to guide us. So, she did what people like her have been trained to do since the dawn of civilization; she preached the benefits of school, religion and god fearing. It was comforting, but not very assuring, especially when coming from someone who wasn't practicing what they were preaching.

This book is for people like me, who know that there is a better way, and that they can do more with their life if given an opportunity.

I purposely wrote it in a "how to" format that explains clearly and precisely what needs to be done in order to achieve success.

My book is designed to take the guesswork out of how to become successful in anything that the mind can dream of.

And here is the best part! Anyone can use it! The spectrum is wide-ranging and all-encompassing, from kids that dream of becoming astronauts and veterinarians, to parents who want a better life for their child. This book will teach them how to succeed!

The Desire to Succeed

There are those of us who are born with an unquenchable desire to succeed. Against unimaginable odds we rise to the top and make a place for ourselves in the halls of success. We become teachers, athletes, ministers, performers, mothers and fathers.

There is a special place for some of us in the media and press, and yes, some of us even become heroes and champions. We carry the burden of setting examples to "wannabees" and aspirants willing to sacrifice sweat, tears, and even blood, on their path to self-prescribed greatness.

Though the torch sometimes gets heavy, and burden gets great , we wouldn't trade it for all the gold in king Midas' tomb. This is a truism that all successful people share, the satisfaction of a job well done cannot be matched when one looks back on their life retrospectively.

To those of you who want to travel the paths of champions and leaders and earn a seat at the table with us at the end of your road, I have written a path for you and yours to get here. Join us, we await your presence, your chair awaits you!

Finally, if you want to see me in action, go to Youtube and type in Theriault vs Batiste. You will see my second world championship match in front of eight thousand screaming fans and millions of viewers on ESPN TV. But, I do have to caution you in advance; the fight was at the end of my career I was dealing with a still painful (recovering) broken hand, and I loss the fight.

Cry not for me though. I had, beaten poverty, made it to the top of the mountain, previously been United States and World Champion, and most importantly, I succeeded !

The Magic of DAGPAW

DAGPAW is the acronym I use to describe the six essential skills necessary to succeed in life. It stands for **D**iscipline, **A**'s & B's, **G**oal setting, **P**erseverance, **A**ttitude, and **W**ork Ethic. I came to this conclusion after reflecting on what it took for me to free myself from a possible life of destruction and become a world champion.

DAGPAW is the standard by which all WCRB karate classes are taught. Although martial arts instructors may articulate it differently, it is also the basis for how professional martial artists teach.

My journey into martial arts started way before I considered making a bid for the world championship. It actually began in the sixties in a small, out-of-the-way karate school that few people knew or heard about.

When I started taking karate very few people knew what it was. Judo was all the rage, right behind boxing as a primary source of self defense. Bruce Lee had not yet made a name for himself, so his impact was not yet felt.

The year was 1967. I was fourteen and running with street gangs. My story is not the average, that of someone being bullied and needing a safety course. On the contrary, I ran with a gang, and though we weren't the kind to have trouble with the law, other kids knew better than to mess with one of us.

One day I got to thinking about how much trouble I would have with other kids if my friends weren't around. This made me concerned for my safety and I started thinking about what my options were.

I'd heard about this new fighting thing called karate. Rumor had it that, if you knew karate, you could take on ten to fifteen people without breaking a sweat.

The next day, I showed up at a karate studio looking to take lessons. The funny thing was, though I wanted to take lessons, it didn't occur to me that I would have to pay for them.

The style was Japanese GoJu, the instructor was Michael Paralgo. Sensei Paralgo was a soft-spoken man, who didn't laugh me out of the studio when I told him that I couldn't pay the fifteen dollar monthly fee. Instead, he gave me a broom, a bucket, and a mop, and made a deal with me to clean the studio for my lessons. This was my introduction to work ethic. I knew that things had to be done right in order for me to continue receiving essons.

Because I was working for my lessons, they became more valuable to me and I didn't take them for granted. I worked hard when I was at the studio, and harder with my free time at home. At green belt – which took about a year to get – I made the decision to become a black belt. Then I wanted to become THE BLACK BELTS' black belt, the person that other black belts aspired to be like.

I didn't know it then, but **DAGPAW** had taken root. I had acquired the beginnings of discipline, perseverance, attitude, goal setting, and work ethic. My life would never be the same again.

Because of my new-found confidence, I no longer ran with gangs. My self-esteem and positive attitude had risen and I started to believe that life had more to offer than being the next generation of street thug. At eighteen I joined the army to make a new life for myself.

While in the army, once again I was exposed to high levels of discipline – only this time it was on a twenty four hour basis. It gave my life purpose and made whatever I was doing more important than other impulses (like excessive partying, night-clubbing and drinking). My life took on a new meaning and had value, which is what I want to share in the passages of this book. But first, an acknowledgment of need-to-know information. Read on...

The Ugly Child Syndrome

We live in the generation of the "ugly child". It has nothing to do with a child's physical features; it has to do with manners, or lack thereof.

Every day, today's generation of children exhibits the kind of defiant, obnoxious, abusive behavior towards adults that was unheard of when I was a child.

I believe that this change in the way that adults and children communicate with each other is in direct response to the "seen and not heard, spare the rod and spoil the child" generation.

Kids who lived through it hated it so much that when they grew up they went completely in the opposite direction and allow their kids unheard-of liberties – not only when they speak to adults, but how they conduct themselves in general.

This, coupled with the legal system's "child abuse" discipline, the parent mentality is wreaking havoc on children of all ages.

For example, how many times have you seen this scenario?

The parent says, "Bobby I want you to stop it right now! Bobby I mean it this time! Bobby you're not listening to me! Okay Bobby, I'm going to start counting. Bobby one, Bobby two," and so on.

Is Bobby deaf? No. He just decided to show off for his friends by embarrassing his mother.

This kind of behavior s not unique, or an isolated incident. Unfortunately, this kind of behavior has become the norm for this generation of child.

It's what I call the "Ugly Child Syndrome".

Since this book is designed to give a parent's child the greatest possibility to succeed, it needs to be addressed, because "ugly children" become "throwaway children".

What I mean is that people who have the power to impact a child's life in profoundly positive ways are increasingly starting to turn their backs on them, essentially throwing their futures away.

I know because I am guilty of it. Here is what happened.

Some time ago, I was coming out of a recreation center where I had a class. When I stepped outside, I saw this boy who looked about nine laying into this girl who looked about twelve.

He called her every profanity he could think of. Forget the fact that it was a girl; this kid let her have it!

He looked over and saw me watching him and without hesitation began to lay into me:" What the f--- you looking at? You old mother f----er. " I shook my head and went on my way.

A couple of months later, his mother brought him to my class. She said, "I'd like you to teach my son karate because his mouth is getting him in trouble."

I looked at him, then looked at my schedule and said, "I'm all booked up. I can put him on a wait list and call you when an opening comes up."

The fact was, I had plenty of space, but after that incident I didn't want anything to do with him. I "threw him away."

And I'm just a Karate instructor!

I've seen it happen on a much higher level.

In the nineties, I was asked to be a mentor to a nine year-old boy. He was getting in all kinds of trouble at school. When he was in the fourth grade, I was being called by the school a couple of times a week to come down to the school to calm him down.

He didn't have ADHD or anything like that; he just didn't want anybody telling him what to do.

I want to stop here for a moment to say that this is one of the great perplexities of life. Here you have a kid who acts out because he doesn't like people telling him what to do. He falls behind, gets bad grades, and grows up working for one of the other kids in his class who becomes his boss and tells him what to do.

You would think that, with a little guidance, he would put his nose to the grindstone and become a boss himself. Go figure.

I would walk into his class and his teacher would be trying to calm him down. She would say things like, "Just give it a try. It's all right. You can do it. Nobody's perfect, etc..."

And in a demonstrative act of total defiance he would shout, "You can't tell me what to do! You're not my mother! Go to h----- etc..." He would totally disrupt the class. This went on the entire school year.

When he got to fifth grade, amazingly, he started his tantrums on his new teacher, only this time his teacher said "Stop right there. If you don't want to do the work, don't worry about it." He said, "put your head down and take a nap. In fact, when we have a test go to the bathroom and take a long time. Stay in there as long as you like, just don't disrupt my class."

The kid was as happy as a hobo with a ham sandwich, because he actually thought that he had won.

He didn't realize that the teacher had just thrown his life away, because when he grows up and tries to get a job his options will be extremely few with a limited education.

The boy and I parted because his mother thought my karate program ate into his playtime.

Martial arts teach self-control, respect for self, and respect for others. Enough said.

DAGPAW Success Tip

1. Control yourself.
2. Respect yourself.
3. Respect others.

What it Means to Succeed

Asking a child, "what does it mean to succeed?" is like asking an adult, "what is the meaning of life?"

They think they know, but are really not sure. In our DAGPAW system we make it very clear that success is accomplishing your stated goal.

In other words, if you say you want to grow up to be a doctor and you do that, you have succeeded. On the other hand, if you say you want to grow up to be a doctor, but you grow up to clean rest rooms, you have not succeeded.

As simply as this concept is to understand, it is extremely difficult to do unless you have had practice doing so.

> *DAGPAW Success Tip*
> **It is the history of small successes that guarantees a large success.**

We look at success like this. Suppose you are seven and never rode a bicycle before. The first time you try to ride it you fall off. The next time you try, you stay on a little longer, and the next time even longer. After a series of determined efforts, you're finally able to ride the bike.

Something that seamed incredibly difficult a short while ago now is easy, and can be done almost effortlessly.

This concept is taught exactly the same way in karate. We award belts of different colors as students increase their skills.

(When a child first comes to a karate studio and sees a Black Belt in action, a lot of them can't imagine themselves being able to do what they see.)

The gold belt – first official belt – is our "fall off the bike stage". (It is also the belt where we experience the most dropouts.)

It is at this level that things seem incredibly hard.

The next level is the green, then purple, blue, red, brown and ultimately the black belt.

As a student gets closer to the black belt, the techniques, though more difficult, become easier to do because of the improved coordination, balance etc. that the student is acquiring along the way.

The difference between learning to ride the bike and learning karate is that in karate the different levels of belt are designed to develop success skills, such as confidence, esteem, perseverance, attitude, and more.

Once a child acquires these skills they should be able to take them anywhere and succeed.

Martial arts classes help kids succeed incrementally, consciously, and learn that by breaking a big task up they can get the job done in a reasonable amount of time, no matter how daunting the job may seem.

Window of Success

Life Span: It is estimated that humans live about eighty year, broken into quarters that's 20, 40, 60, 80.

My approach to instilling success skills works best like this: the first twenty years you should be acquiring success skills, the second twenty years should be acquiring things: wife/husband, car, home, kids etc., the third twenty years should be planning for retirement, and the last quarter should be enjoying retirement.

So far not much new has been said. Most people instinctively try to follow those guidelines.

Here is where my program differs.

If you take the first quarter (twenty years) and break it into quarters again, here is where you'll find the real impact is made.

By breaking the first quarter up you now have: 5, 10, 15, and 20.

Between ages three and five is where you should start imparting success skills into your child.

Up to year five children learn by being allowed to explore and experiment. They need to be allowed to roam freely, touch, feel, and manipulate the world around them.

They are not ready for a heavy load of discipline and structure.

In fact, introducing toddlers to **_rigid_** discipline concepts too early can have a completely opposite effect on what you are trying to do; instead, what you would have a toddler do should more appropriately be called **_"disciplay!"_**

Disciplay is learning discipline concepts while playing. (I know it sounds oxymoronic, but it can be done with a little effort.)

On the other hand three- to five- year olds readily absorb messages of goal setting, perseverance – and most importantly, leadership, independence, and responsibility.

What you're trying to do is place your child in a position so they will grow into leading others.

This will keep them safe and allow him/her to be the one to determine their destination as they get older, instead of following poor associated examples.

At the age of about nine to early teens, most kids start hanging around in groups like schools of fish.

At that point it gets harder and harder for them to warm to your ideas about their future.

They start to acquire a group mentality and lose their individualism.

Whatever the leader of the group thinks is cool is what they will do.

At age three to five, most children's minds are open to suggestions because there are no competing forces.

Humans are funny creatures. Most look for someone to give them guidance.

We gravitate towards people with independence and leadership qualities.

Whether they lead a group of kids or not is irrelevant, you want your kids to develop leadership qualities, so that what they are doing – getting good grades, playing piano, taking karate etc. – is looked at by other kids as cool. That way, they won't be jeered into following a leader with bad character.

Most parents are so caught up in teaching their children to get good grades that they don't look at the big picture; good grades without leadership skills are why kids who get good grades get labeled as nerds.

The Age of Choices

At my school we start to teach the importance of making good choices at age three with this rhyme: "Choices, choices good and bad. Bad choices make me said; good choices make me glad."

DAGPAW Success Tip

Choices, choices, good and bad:
Bad choices make me sad;
Good choices make me glad.

Again, if you look at the life span scale that I demonstrated in the last passage, the first twenty years are pivotal in the choices that people make.

I know a person that just got his voting rights back at age sixty five because of a bad choice that he made in his late teens.

If your child gets marred with a criminal record, their ability to be successful is a l but lost.

I recommend that you start early to help your child to understand the importance of making good decisions.

We do this with the WCRB Karate "Student Pledge".

The Student Pledge

We strive to conduct ourselves in a manner with honor, integrity, and trust.

To maintain pride in our skills with respect for law and order.

Never to use the things we learn in an abusive or reckless way.

To set a standard of excellence and become an example to follow

In the spirit of THE MARTIAL ARTS

Youth is an opportunity to make choices you won't regret when you grow old.

Discipline: The D in DAGPAW

Discipline: The King of Success Skills

Discipline is the king of success skills, because without it four of the other success skills (goal setting and acquisition, perseverance, getting A's & B's, work ethic) cannot be done.

Kids and Military Influence

Martial arts is an umbrella term that encompasses karate, kung fu, judo, take kwon do, among others. It means military way.

The term martial art came about when self defense skills where mandated in the armies of Japan, Korea, and China.

It wasn't until karate, kung fu, judo and tae kwon do were incorporated into the military that they developed their highly disciplined doctrines.

It is the military's need for control under fire that caused instructors to root discipline into the teachings of what is now known as martial arts.

This method of teaching was compounded when American soldiers began training in martial arts in Okinawa, Korea, and Japan.

When soldiers returned home with black belts ready to teach, they naturally taught the way they learned, with high levels of concentrated effort and discipline.

The reason they did this was twofold: first, discipline makes teaching large groups easier; second: at that time martial arts was only learned in anticipation of a fight or self defense situation.

In the 60's, when I started, martial arts enjoyed a large influx of adult men joining its ranks who wanted to learn how to protect themselves and their families.

(Bruce lee and Chuck Norris where making a big splash.)

By the 70's, when the martial arts began to transition into a sport with more and more non-optional tournament participation required by instructors, adult participation began to drop off.

As the drop rate began to intensify, children who were being bullied began to show up in studios more and more. Although academic studies of the time had not made the connection, parents of bullied children were very aware of their child's in ability to get good grades for fear that the bullying would increase.

Soon, it became apparent that, among the children who were not getting good grades because of bullying, those who started martial arts began to improve their grades.

Parent after parent began singing the praises of martial arts.

More specifically, they praised how the discipline that their child acquired to help them fend off an attack actually helped them get good grades.

This opened the floodgates to a whole new industry.

In martial arts as in the army, **DISCIPLINE** can be defined as "making your body do something it doesn't want to do at that time".

This axiom for fighting accidentally, spilled over into academics and started producing good grades.

Because of discipline, kids started voluntarily staying home to do their homework instead of hanging with friends outdoors.

Kids and Discipline: A Strange Relationship

Have you ever been in a marching band?

I have. It was one of the most rewarding experiences of my life. Showing up at practice and having the head instructor bark out commands: stand up straight, shoulders back, left turn, right turn etc.

It was exhilarating! And once again, the stricter the disciplinarian, the more important the task becomes.

Insistence on discipline while doing a task gives the job more value and importance. When completed, you earn the satisfactory feeling of a job well done. Who doesn't want that!

Most kids resist and complain, but instinctively gravitate towards highly disciplined environments.

The reason is because the structure of a disciplined environment makes kids feel safe.

No one, especially a child, will do well in a helter skelter, chaotic environment.

Those types of environments create fear and uncertainty. Structure creates certainty and safety.

Outwardly, kids may resent discipline, but down inside they want and need it.

The Importance of "Sir and Ma'am"

No other tool teaches self-discipline faster than the insistence of "Sir" or "Ma'am" placed before or after a word.

A simple "Yes, Sir "or "Yes, Ma'am" changes the dynamics of a conversation.

The person speaking the words instinctively understands that they are the subordinate in the discussion and that the person they are addressing is deserving of respect, and most importantly, leadership trust (a willingness to go along with what they are saying).

This is not something to be taken lightly when you are trying to infuse success skills into someone's life, especially if they are not related to you (as in the army, military school, karate class etc.)

Leadership trust is not given lightly.

It must be earned with examples of the person asking for it having done the thing they're asking.

Standard proof of status deserving of leadership trust includes trophies, plaques, medals, resumes, certificates etc.

Fortunately, parents don't have a burden of proof. Their position in a particular instance is accepted-in most cases-simply by being the parent.

Unwittingly though, a lot of parents give up the leadership role and become subordinate to their children by allowing the child to be on the same level as they are by interaction on a first name basis.

After 40 years of working with children, it is my belief that, in order to instill leadership skills in your child, you must be the captain of your ship, and steer a course to success with a clear *I'm in charge* doctrine. "Sir and Ma'am" will help do that for you.

Getting your child to say "Sir or Ma'am" to you at home is not as difficult as it may seem.

We get our three year olds and up "Jamboree "class to say "Sir or Ma'am" to their parents by giving them classroom credit for extending courtesy at home. See the Courtesy Champion Card in Appendix A.

One final note: Do not start this part of the program until you are totally committed to its consistency.

Starting and stopping the use of "Sir or Ma'am" will confuse the child and make it seem more like a punishment than a developmental aid.

Discipline Made Easy

How does one instill discipline, unless you are in the military? Force in not the answer.

For purposes of this discussion, there are three types of discipline: Mind control, time control, and body control.
- Mind control discipline is remembering to say things: "Yes sir/Ma'am".
- Time control discipline is having to do something at a certain time: 7:am time to get up, 12 noon time to eat, 9pm time to go to bed, etc
- Body control discipline is making your body do something it doesn't want to do; the key is to do it immediately when asked: sit up, stand still etc

Of the three, "time control" discipline is the easiest because you can be assisted by a clock, friend, relative (mommy, daddy) etc.

Because of its ease, "time control discipline" should be used to introduce young children (3-5) and sensitive kids to discipline.

While an argument can be made that ***all discipline is mental*** we must remain aware that what we are trying to do is find a way to teach discipline to young children who in many cases have not yet acquired awareness.

The easiest way to do this is to break the teaching into three specific components: Time can be used to trigger the mental to control the physical.

Once an individual reaches a certain age of awareness the mental can be used to trigger the time and the physical.

Example: You wake up in the morning and say to yourself, "I have to remember to do this or that at twelve today".

Earlier I stated that "Discipline is making your body do something it doesn't want to do at that time".

If you agree with that statement, then developing an ACTION PLAN to instill discipline into kids is really easier than one might think.

All you have to do is place a time frame on things that need to get done anyway.

For example, instead of letting your child do their homework scattershot, any time they want to, develop a specific time designated especially for homework.

If your child is old enough to do chores, assign a specific time to do them.

The list of things that can be specifically timed is endless i.e. brush their teeth, take out trash, do homework, walk the dog, do the laundry, wash dishes, etc.

The key to making the program work is your ability to not only hold firm on time frames, but to add more as your child gets older. It's what I call the discomfort of success.

By helping your child understand that all members of the family must do their part to make each other's life easier, they will readily volunteer to be given the responsibility of a task that must be done in a timely manner.

As a species, we are reward driven. Every day we go about our day doing things that we otherwise would not do, in anticipation of a reward: go to school (grow up and get a good job), learn to ride a bike (freedom of mobility), don't cross the street on a red light (not get injured), eat our vegetables (run faster and not get sick), etc.

What you want to do is make sure that the reward is consistent with success and is age appropriate – things like:
- More independence
- More responsibility
- Extended play

Here are some examples of how to instill discipline into a growing child:

Preschool	Age: 3-5
Type of Discipline	Timed *disciplay* (loosely structured discipline)
Dinner Time Chores	remove their plate from the table
Bedtime Chores	say their prayers at bedtime
Morning/Night Chores	brush his/her teeth in the morning and at night
Self-Discipline	no playing at nap time or bedtime
Rewards	ice cream, cake or pizza on Saturday afternoon

Elementary to Middle School	Age: 6-13
Type of Discipline	Un- negotiated structure
Chores	Sat wash car and cut grass
	Feed and walk family pet
Self-Discipline	Homework done at specific time
	No phone calls after a certain time
	When street lights come on, come home
	Can't visit certain web sites
Rewards	allowance, allowed to wear haircut of their liking, allowed to stay up all night on Sat or Fri

High School	Age: 14-18
Type of Discipline	Negotiated structure (At this point you might try allowing them to make good choices.)
Chores	Maintain a light or weekend job
	Feed and walk family pet
	Do their own laundry regularly
	Do household laundry once a week
Self-Discipline	No leaving dishes in room
	Lights out at a reasonable hour
	Keep their room clean
	Cut grass or shovel snow without being told
	Help with cooking or cook family dinner once a week
Rewards	More independence

Remember to start small, grow larger, and regularly acknowledge a job well done.

Double Whammy!

People gravitate towards individuals with leadership qualities.

When your child gets old enough you may entertain the idea of getting them a pet that they must solely take care of, e.g. a cat, dog, fish, hamster or turtle.

Not only will this help with the discipline of feeding and cleaning up after them, but it will also instill responsibility, which is at the core of good leadership.

The To Do List

One of the ways that my staff and I have been able to EXTEND discipline from our class to home is with a "To Do List" for six year olds and up.

The list is located on the back of our student's "Class Card".

It lists three things that have to be done every day: make your bed, put your stuff away, and do your homework.

Students must do those three things unsupervised. Once done, they must take their "Class Card" to their parents and have them sign off on completion of their work.

Parents rave about this portion of our program.

They absolutely cannot believe how their child will do those three things everyday without being told, and do them in an organized fashion.

The reason they do it is because we tie our "To Do List" to their belt test.

Students must demonstrate responsibility before they can move on. An example of a "To Do List" is in Appendix B.

By using a little creativity you can create your own home program. Try tying your home program to an allowance, or a birthday or holiday present.

A's and B's: the First A in DAGPAW

Why is it important to get them?

Without looking forward, answer this question, why is it important to get A's and B's? You'd be surprised at how many people don't know. Admittedly, I didn't until I was in my late 30's.

All I knew is that I was told to get A's and B's by my mother, who was told by her mother, who was told by her mother and so on.

It's like the story of shaving both sides of ham off before cooking it for Christmas dinner.

At Christmas dinner preparation a young girl noticed her mother slice both sides of a large ham off before cooking it.

Intrigued she asked, "Mom, why do you cut both sides of the ham off before you cook it?"

Her mother replied, "I never thought of it, but that's the way my mother always cooked it".

At the dinner table with her grandmother present she asked, "Grandma, why do you cut both side of the ham off before you cook it?"

Her grandmother replied, "I never thought of it, but that's the way my mother always cooked it."

On summer vacation down south at the family home she came into contact with her great grandmother and asked,

"Gran Gran, why do you cut both sides of a ham off before cooking it?"

Gran Gran looked at her with a smile and said, "When I was young, we didn't have a pan large enough to cook the whole thing."

Like repeating your parents, who repeated their parents, who repeated their parent's wishes for their child to get good grades, some habits are hard to break.

The reality, though, is this, A's and B's equal choices. The more A's & B's you get, the more job, and college choices you have.

In our classes when we explain this to our students they are hugely receptive and eagerly follow up by bringing in their report cards quarterly as requested.

A's & B's: How to Guarantee Your Child Gets Them

In our classes, not only do we explain to children why it's important to get A's and B's, we teach our kids how to get A's and B's.

It's a three step process. Here is what we do.

We teach our kids **how, when, and why** to concentrate.

Study after study demonstrates that most kids that don't do well in school have an inability to concentrate for sustained periods of time.

No sooner does the teacher start talking, some kids start looking out the window or engaging playfully with a classmate.

We've learned how to nip this behavior in the bud. When one of our instructors begins a class he/she shouts "Cheerio" (The Korean word for attention).

The class snaps to the attention position and says loudly, "CONCENTRATE".

The instructor then says, "Meaning?" (Which can be deciphered as **how?**)

The kids as a group respond, "focus with my eyes, focus with my brain, focus with my ears, and focus with my body, Sir/Ma'am!"

The instructor pushes forward with the question, "And focus means?"

The students respond by saying, "Keep it still" The instructor then asks, "**When** do you CONCENTRATE?"

The students respond by saying "Whenever a teacher is talking,, Sir/Ma'am!"

Finally, the instructor asks, "**Why** do you CONCENTRATE?"

The students respond by saying, "So that you can remember what is being said, Sir/Ma'am."

Periodically the instructor will ask, "How do you keep your eyes still?"

The students say, "Look at the person who is talking."

How do you keep your brain still?"

The students say, "Think about what is being said."

Sometimes he/she might ask, "How do you keep your ears still?"

The students say, "Look at the person who is talking to you Sir/Ma'am."

Magic? Not really.

Well thought out and results getting? ABSOLUTELY!

One of my pet beliefs is that **people who understand why they are being asked to do something are not just more likely to do it, they will do it well.**

So far, formatting the start of my classes like this has proven me right!

Since we started having our instructors start classes like this, the improvement in our student's grades have skyrocketed!

This experiment is hugely successful.

By teaching our kids **HOW, WHY and WHEN to CONCENTRATE,** they are able to zero in on specific information pertaining to tests, quizzes, standardized tests (Virginia SOL's) you name it, and retain it for later use.

Some Parents have even noticed an improvement in note taking, which is vital in the transportation of important thoughts and ideas from the class to home.

But let's face it, not all children are going to be able to grasp ideas like concentration and focus.

So for the little ones we teach a simple equation: "Good homework equals good tests; good tests equals good grades."

Try it, it works.

DAGPAW Success Tip
Good Homework = Good Tests **Good Tests = Good Grades**

Goal Setting: the G in DAGPAW

Goal Setting and Acquisition

If "Discipline "is the "King" of success skills, then goal setting is the "Queen".

The only way that success can be acquired without discipline and goal setting is by winning the lottery (not likely).

Goal setting is working towards achieving something until you complete it.

Humans are goal setters by nature.

The problem is most of us do it instinctively, not consciously.

It is the conscious acquisition of goals that makes us successful.

Every time a child says, "I'm going to save money to buy something" or "I'm going to surprise my parents by getting a good report card" they are goal setting.

But unless they have a plan of action, goal setting is mostly wishful thinking. This brings me to my next point.

Goal Setting: The Five Essential Elements

In order for goal setting to work, the goal must have these five essential elements:

1) **It must be yours**: Goals cannot be bestowed upon you by someone else. For example: A loving parent looks at their daughter and says, "When you grow up you're going to be the best ballet dancer on the planet. " As soon as the girl gets eighteen she says,

"I love you dearly mom and dad but I always wanted to be a jockey and race horses."

2) **It must be realistic**: If your child told you that they were going to learn to fly like "Superman" by age of eleven you'd break out laughing and say good luck.

   On the other hand, if they told you they wanted to grow up and work for the "Peace Corp" saving starving children, you'd know that with hard work and determination they could do it.

3) **It must be important**: Someone trying to accomplish a goal must be willing to sacrifice having fun for hard work and determination.

4) **It must have a time frame** of short-, intermediate- and long-range ending points:

   Saying that you are going to be a doctor one day is open ended and subject to chance. Saying that you are going to finish high school at seventeen (short-range), college by twenty-one (mid-range), medical school by twenty-five and become a doctor by twenty-seven (long-range) puts a sense of urgency and realism to the proposition.

5) Lastly and most importantly, *a goal must have an Action Plan*.

   Having an Action Plan will force you to ask yourself tough questions about how you plan to get the thing done, e.g. where will financing come from, how much education you will need, etc.

Goal setting must be broken down into bite-sized manageable pieces, with every small success leading to the larger success.

In my class we teach this concept with our belt system.

We teach kids that their long range goal is the black belt, their mid-range goal is the purple belt, and their short-range goal is their first graduation belt, the gold belt.

We then further break the process down by saying that they have three months (48 practice sessions. 24 in class and 24 at home) to achieve the goal of earning the next belt.

Their class card provides the "Action Plan". (See Appendix C for an example of the Class Card.) Once the goal, time frame, and action plan have been developed, achievement check points are established in the form of stripes on their belt.

A typical gold belt acquisition looks like this: after the first month (eight lessons) a gold stripe is placed on their belt; after the second month (sixteen lessons) another gold stripe is placed on their belt; after the third month (twenty four lessons) they are ready to test for the gold belt.

The process is then repeated through every level until the student achieves the rank of black belt.

You can teach these concepts to your child yourself at home it's really not that hard.

Just remember the five "must haves". Pick a subject, and get started it's as simple as that.

For those of you that don't have the time or resources to teach your child goals acquisition, I highly recommend that you take your child to the neighborhood martial arts school and let them do it. They are the professionals at it, and most will do a great job.

You can always tell a quality studio – they are the ones with the introductory or trial program of some kind. Let's move on.

Goal Setting: Plus One More (Sometimes) Essential Element

Before I go to the next part of DAGPAW, I need to touch on an important part of goal setting that is not always necessary. I call it, the "plus one" essential element because it's not always needed. It is finding out what you need to know and by when you need to know it!

All goals have this category, but most goals can be acquired without conscious use of it. For example, if I'm a child my goal might be to get my parents to allow a friend to sleep over on the weekend. The need-to-know information is if my parents are the kind of people who let kids outside the family stay over.

Most kids don't give that question a second thought, they just begin schmoosing their parent's at the beginning of the week, and close to the end of the week they pop the question. Their parent's either say yes or no and everyone moves on.

As a child, most of your goal setting encounters happen just like that. They have no rhyme or reason and you, more than likely, have no guidance to help you along.

So you, like everyone else, begin your journey into goal setting completely unknowledgeable about how to guarantee success!

Some people, through hard work and determination, are able to make goal setting work. But not every goal has to be HARD WORK!

The process can be made considerably easier with a working knowledge of my five plus one essential elements.

For some goals, trying to accomplish them without the "plus one" essential element is like trying to do something that you don't know how to do. You can't drive a car if you never took lessons, nor can you swim, ski or fly an airplane. You have to be schooled before the task can be performed. With some goals it's the same thing.

Essentially, the greater the benefit attached to the goal, the more educated about it you have to be.

Unlike having a friend spend the night, if I wanted to become a doctor, not only would the goal have to be important, be mine, be realist, have a time frame, and have an action plan, but I would also have to figure out what I need to know and by when I need to know it.

Let's say that I am in the fourth or fifth grade and I decide that I want to become a doctor, the process would look like this (this example is poorly hypothetical and should not be used on its own):

Suppose I decide that I want to become a doctor.

1. Either by internet, asking a guidance counselor, or calling a doctor friend's office, I acquire the following information:
    a. The amount of and what kind of schooling I would need to have
    b. What kind of grades I need to have
    c. How much money it will cost

2. The plan might look like this:

a. Get in the habit of getting A's and B's in school (It's hard to suddenly start getting good grades if you are not used to it.)
b. While in high school find out if there are any apprenticeship programs that will allow me to start networking in the industry
c. Find out what college best prepares kids for medical school
d. Find out what kind of grades I will need to get nto the college
e. Find out how much the college will cost and if they have scholarships for things that I might start trying to qualify for
f. Find out if there is grant or set aside money I might get from a government program for medical school and college
g. Figure out what kind of job I would need that will pay me a salary that will allow me to go to school and pay for living expenses
h. Put together time table and action plan
i. Get to work

If I don't have financing, the same kind of planning might have to be done for medical school.

Some of you might be thinking, wait a minute, a fourth or fifth grader doesn't think like that, and to that I say YOU'RE RIGHT!

The purpose of this book is to not just teach you how to teach your child how to think like that, but show them how to do it.

Remember, by using the "Window of Success" guideline some of you will be able to begin the process of teaching your child success skill as early as three.

With a background of conscious small goals acquisitions your child should be ready and willing to welcome the challenge of this larger more important one at the appropriate age.

The key is confidence through continuity!

If you've infused your child with DAGPAW concepts at an early age, he/she might surprise you by accomplishing unbelievable things by the time they become young adults.

The next necessary skill is....

Perseverance: the P in DAGPAW

If human beings are anything, we are creatures of habit.

It is during the "Window of Success" years that we develop the traits that make us who we are when we grow up.

Unwittingly, as a child, a lot of us develop habits that guarantee failure as an adult.

And unbeknownst to our parents at the time, they compound the situation by trying to make us happy.

One of the worst habits that a parent can allow a child to develop is a habit to give up/quit all the time.

During the early years of my martial arts competition days, a writer (Dr. A. Jose Jones) from *"Official Karate"* was doing a story about me.

As we sat and talked about my rise to prominence in the East Coast point tournament circuit, he asked me what was the single most important thing I had done to secure my position as a highly rated fighter?

Without hesitation I said, "Conquered the quitting impulse." That became the title of the article.

Every day children all over the world are allowed to quit doing something when it gets hard – or worse, when it stops being fun.

You can see the quitting habit rear its head as early as seven when kids first take up t- ball or become football *"ankle biters"*.

Here is a typical scenario: Child – mommy, daddy please, please let me join the football team. I'll do anything, clean my room etc. Parent- okay Bobby, just as long as you're having fun.

Two weeks later the child quits. Why? Because he wasn't having fun anymore.

About a month later he starts again, please mommy daddy, please let me join the soccer team, I'll do anything you ask, clean my room for a week.

Mom and dad... okay Bobby, anything you want as long as you're having fun.

A few weeks later the child is allowed to quit. Why? Because he wasn't having fun.

Some parents, for some reason, think that if their child isn't having fun, they shouldn't be ***made*** to do it.

I see it all the time – not just in my karate class, but industry wide. In martial arts most dropouts occur at the gold belt beginner level. That is when the training stops being fun all of the time.

In helping a student overcome his/her impulse to quit I remind them that, "If it's worth having, it's not always going to be fun".

Becoming a doctor or professional athlete is going to take a lot of hard work.

It's best to buckle down and learn how to finish what you start at an early age. Then, if you still don't like what you are doing after you accomplish it, go ahead and quit then.

Learning to quit if you're not having fun at an early age is disastrous to goals accomplishment.

If it's worth having, it's not going to be easy, and may not be fun. On the other hand, there is great happiness in accomplishing one's goals.

A Case for Finishing What You Start

I started doing martial arts when I was fourteen. Over the years, I became very good at it. Sometime in the ninth grade, I started to have ambitions of becoming a martial arts superstar like Bruce Lee or Chuck Norris.

I decided that in order to do that, I had to become the Black Belts' Black Belt – the person that other Black Belts would look up to and aspire to be like. In order to do that, I had to become a world champion.

As my dream went, once I became champion I would have all the things that champions had: fame, wealth, fast cars, women etc. I also started believing that fighters didn't have a need to be super-educated and that I could get away with a modicum of schooling because, after all, how smart do you have to be to fight?

In order to accelerate my journey to stardom, I made the decision to drop out of school so that I could concentrate solely on my plan.

Weeks became months, months became years. Through hard work and determination, I did it! I won the title and became champion of the world.

Shortly after I became champion things started to happen just like I had planned. I acquired a certain amount of wealth, had a fast car, a house, and a beautiful wife.

One day I received an offer from the office of then-Mayor Marion Barry of Washington DC. He was putting together a program called the "Roving Leaders", and would have area champions Ivan LaBray (Washington Capitals), Wes Unsel (Washington Bullets), and myself tour the city, giving lectures and seminars on how we became champions.

I was ecstatic! Everything that I have ever wanted was about to come true. I quickly signed on!

I'll never forget the first week of the tour because it was the worse week of my life. I was an embarrassment to the Mayor's office. Because I had dropped out of school, my English was so bad that sixth graders were correcting me in the middle of a sentence.

I mean... I was not pronouncing "th" at the end of words, my enunciation, and elocution was zip. To say I was inarticulate would be putting it mildly. I was literally a laughing stock of a representative for the Mayor's office.

That was the week I decided to go back to school, and at twenty-one, I was the oldest high school student in my class. I should have finished school the first time around, but I let grandiose ideas cloud my thinking.

Attitude: The Second A in DAGPAW

What You Think Matters

Someone once said, "If you think you're going to win, or if you think you're going to lose, you are right!"

Having a positive attitude is fuel for goals accomplishment. It is to your thoughts what gas is to a car, the energy that keeps it going. It is also the force behind getting things done.

A positive attitude has, metaphorically, allowed man to move mountains, but what exactly is it?

Simply put, it's what I call the, I CAN DO IT! syndrome.

People who have it attack a problem with a "I can do it, let me try it, when's my turn, get out of my way" mentality; people who don't approach a problem – instead of attack a problem – with a "I don't know, you go, what if it doesn't work" mentality.

The difference is supreme confidence over fear and indecision.

The question is, where does it come from?

Why do some people rise to the occasion while others slink away?

The answer is failure, or how you've been wired to deal with it.

Some people are so afraid to fail that they won't give certain things a try, while others take a loss in stride and "pick themselves up" and have at it again.

Thomas Edison (the light bulb), the Wright brothers, Orville and Wilbur (the plane), Christopher Columbus (America): these are just a few people who made major mistakes before they got things right.

We are growing into a society that is afraid of letting our children make mistakes.

We have Little League, basketball, football etc., where every team is a winner; there are no losers anymore.

Everyone gets a "participation trophy".

Where will inner strength come from if nobody ever overcomes a loss?

Think about it, some athlete's most defining moments are when they overcome a defeat and come back from a loss.

Before I started winning, I was losing all the time. But I, like other champions-to-be, had a "Never say die attitude." I knew deep down inside that I could do it – I just had to figure out how.   When I did, it was game on.

Parents, don't protect your kids from themselves.

They'll surprise you with their tenacity. With a little encouragement, one day you'll start hearing them say (about the other team), "We'll fix them next time".

Work Ethic: the W in DAGPAW

Work ethic is the amount of effort you put into a job that you have been assigned to do, and it's totally mental, and sometimes it can trump A's & B's.

Example: Let's say I have a child, and I say to the child, "Bobby, I want you to go up stairs, clean your room, make your bed, feed the cat, and wash the toilet". In most cases the response would, "Man this SUCKS, I hate dad, why do I always have to do the tough stuff, etc."

On the other hand, suppose I say, "Bobby, I want you to go up stairs, clean your room, make your bed, feed the cat, and wash the toile. And when you finish we're going to have a pizza party with ice and cake."

This time the response might be, "Oh boy, this is great! You're the greatest dad ever."

What's changed?

The reward at the end is the difference. Because of it, Bobby will approach the job with a totally different mindset.

This attitude difference causes huge problems on job sites nationwide, and sometimes causes people with high work ethics to outperform people with A's & B's.

Parents encouraging students to get good grades must also encourage a strong work ethic.

Example: Bobby and Johnny are in the same class. Bobby, gets all A's. Johnny struggles along, sometimes getting A's and sometimes getting C's and B minuses. They graduate and get a job working at the same place.

Bobby, comes to work late and leaves early, is argumentative with the boss, does sloppy unprofessional work, and all of his coworkers hate him.

Johnny, gets to work early and stays late, is supportive of the boss's goals, when given a job he finishes it on time or early, conducts himself professionally at all times, volunteers to stay late when needed all of his coworkers love him and he's a team player.

One day, because of budget cuts, the boss has to let one of them go. Which one do you think it will be? Answer: Goodbye Mr. A's and B's.

There are hundreds, maybe thousands, of examples of how some person who couldn't get good grades starts a dog walking, grass cutting or carpet/office cleaning service and makes millions of dollars.

The fact is that not al kids can get all A's in every subject all the time. I couldn't.

But that's okay; there are millions of dollars to be made in "low tech" jobs for those who have a strong work ethic.

Teach DAGPAW Like a Master

If I were to take a group of, let's say, five people and say, "I want everyone to think of the color blue". I would have five different shades of blue, e.g. aqua marine, royal, light blue, powder, etc.

On the other hand, if I say, "okay everyone think of royal blue", only then would I have all five people thinking of the color that I want.

Teaching is the exact same thing. Everyone is different. Good teachers know this, and plan their lessons accordingly. I highly suggest that you take the time to get to know how your child learns.

Some people learn better verbally, some visually; some are a combination of both. Some people have very high attention spans, some very low.

For the best results you must take the time to figure out how your child learns best! Once you do your child will look forward to working with you and be receptive to your overtures.

Being one of three children, my mother tried to teach us the times tables the exact same way. We weren't allowed to use our fingers, a pencil or any other aid. We were made to memorize the answers and expected to know them by heart.

It was traumatic and awful. My mind just didn't work that way, I shut down constantly, and often froze when it became my turn to give an answer. In order to get me to perform my mother began spanking me, punishing me, not letting me have dinner, and making me stay up after bedtime until I was able to regurgitate the answers.

That was the way that people taught in those days. It produced good intentions but poor results.

The other thing about that style of teaching is that it destroys the parent / child bond of feeling safe and instills fear and apprehension into the learning environment. The funny thing is, back in the sixties, the teachers were doing the same thing in school – punishing kids for not being able to learn in the prescribed manner.

Above all, you do not want your child to develop a fear of talking to you about things that are important to them. This happens when you have an overzealous, impatient teaching style.

Children learn better in safe, comfortable, fun, learning environments of encouragement and confidence in them, environments that produce a "you can do this, I support you" feeling.

Be patient! Your child is not an adult and your child is not you. He/she will have their own way of seeing the world and learning. You must figure out what it is.

Let's Get Started

Parents, you have now been armed with the tools to make your child hugely successful.

What say you? Are you ready to hit the ground running and get the job done?

From this point, there are three options in order to do the program:

1) You can take the information that you have digested and design your own home program.

2) With a small investment you can purchase one of our home study programs that includes backup support.

3) If you live in the Washington D.C. area you can sign your child up for Master Batiste's class at the Arlington Parks and Recreation Centers: 703-228-4747. If you live outside the area, you can seek a martial arts school that ascribes to the DAGPAW curriculum and teaching methods.

What Parents Say about DAGPAW

I am pleased to fully endorse WCRB karate, a program designed and taught by World Champion Master Rodney Batiste. His program emphasizes a goal based approach to learning karate through discipline, respect for oneself and others, academic achievement and dedication to improvement.

I have watched my son grow through this program. Master Batiste's ability to enthusiastically explain and demonstrate new skills to children, coupled with his program's blueprint for success, has helped my then 4 year-old evolve into a confident, capable and respectful 6 year-old. Through this program, he has been given the tools to succeed as he enters his early school years.

In the introductory class, "Tiny Tigers" my 4 year-old was unsure of being around larger groups, of demonstrating techniques in front of others and of learning something new through instruction. Now he eagerly participates in the learning process and has graduated on to new challenges.

My wife and I look forward to enrolling our younger sons in the same program. I whole-heartedly recommend the WCRB program without any hesitation to all parents who want to bring out the best in their children and setting them up for a successful and fulfilling life.

Sincerely,

Jim Evans and Diana Hung

The DAGPAW teaching approach helps kids develop the skills to be successful. The primary and most important skill that everybody should develop is Discipline and realizing it is simply "making your body do something it doesn't want to do" puts a new perspective to the term as a self-management skill. Additionally important are the development of the skills related to A's & B's which opens the doors for future opportunities, Perseverance teaches to overcome challenges, Attitude to develop positive behavior, and Work Ethic which develops a person's character as they display integrity, responsibility, and quality. The most impressive skill taught is Goal Setting via the Class Card which provides a visual map guiding kids on how they can accomplish their next goal in WCRB, however the structure is very relevant in teaching them how to accomplish any goal in life. It really is never too early to teach the skill of goal setting!

As parents, we really appreciate the DAGPAW teaching approach because the skills mirror what we also try to teach at home. Therefore, it feels like a partnership for ensuring our kids succeed not only with martial arts, but in every aspect of their entire life.

Gail Thomas

I am the mom of two boys, two-years apart in age. Both are involved in various competitive sports and are very active. At age 4 I enrolled each of them in Master Batiste's beginning karate classes. I was looking to inspire discipline and listening skills, but what they got out of it was so much more than that. Master Batiste clearly outlined his expectations for behavior - not only in class - but also at school and at home. And then, he routinely held them accountable for their behavior. He emphasized to the children that they are capable and able to contribute to their household. He not only inspired discipline in my boys, but also perseverance. Learning new skills in karate is not easy. Many of the moves are controlled and require focus and practice. This is a difficult task for any new participant, but especially so for young children. Master Batiste has the ability to encourage each child - regardless of ability - to keep working hard and to do so with a good attitude. It's a great foundation for kids to have in place for life long goal setting - hard work and perseverance creates positive results. What I did not expect when I enrolled my boys in karate class was that it would impact our family life as well. The ideas that the boys were learning in class became part of our parenting style and we continue to use these strategies as they grow. I would highly recommend utilizing Master Batiste's techniques and strategies for instilling life skills in your child by using karate as a guide. It really works!

Abby Kurtz

APPENDIX A: COURTESY CHAMPION CARD

What Is Courtesy?

At WCRB Karate we say that, "Courtesy is using good manner to get people to do things for you."

Example: If you dropped something and looked at the person next to you and yelled out," HEY YOU! Pick that up." The person you are talking to will probably ignore you. On the other hand, if you dropped something and looked at the person next to you and respectfully said, "Would you get that for me please?" They would probably do it.

There are many kinds of courtesies. There is: Class room courtesy (also called classroom etiquette), bathroom courtesy, courtesy in sports, courtesy at the movies, courtesy at the water fountain etc. The list is endless.

Courtesy in a classroom would mean: sitting up straight and paying attention instead of ignoring the person talking, raising your hand when you have a question, not interrupting the speaker and not entering the room noisily etc.

Using courtesy in the bathroom would include: not leaving the toilet seat up, rinsing out the sink after brushing your teeth, using air freshener after using the toilet, and hurrying out if someone is waiting.

Here are four places that you can teach your child how to use a different kind of courtesy:
- Water fountain: ladies first, don't spit in fountain; don't stay to long if others are waiting.

- Getting into a car: hold the door for someone, offer to let someone sit next to the window, don't distract driver with loud noise or talking.
- Dinner table: don't chew with mouth open, use a napkin to remove unwanted food from mouth, don't reach across table for things, ask if anyone would like the last of something before you take it, compliment the cook, don't forget to say thank when eating at a friend's house.
- Sharing bedroom with sibling: don't turn lights on when you enter the room, don't play loud music when others are trying to sleep, enter and leave room quietly, cover yourself while moving around room, leave smelly sneakers outdoors.

As you go about the first twelve weeks of the courtesy challenge, the most important thing is to be honest with your child's use of courtesy and have fun!

How to use Courtesy Champion Card
- Write Tiger's name on front of card.
- Choose the word "Courtesy "by circling it.
- Each day your child uses courtesy, place a smiley face in the box that represents the day of the week.
- Your child must get five smiley faces in a seven-day week.
- At the end of the week, circle a smiley face or unhappy face for how well he/she has done.
- At the end of week four, give him/her a "Courtesy" badge if they received four smiley faces in a row.
- Repeat process, only this time, when he/she gets to week four award him/her a star.
- After the final four weeks award him/her the "Tiny Tiger" badge.
- After twelve weeks, move on to "Respect", twelve more weeks move to "Discipline".

Tiny Tigers Karate Team

WCRB On-Site Karate

Courtesy Champion Card

This session I am working on:

Courtesy   Discipline   Respect

Score: 1 2 3 4 5 6 7 8 9 10

Tigers
Name:_____

At the end of program, send this card in to:
WCRB Karate
P.O. Box 7450, Arlington, VA 22207 to receive
A FREE "Tiny Tiger Headband"

Week	Mon	Tue	Wed	Thu	Fri	Sat	Sun	
1								☺ ☹
2								☺ ☹
3								☺ ☹
4								☺ ☹
5								☺ ☹
6								☺ ☹
7								☺ ☹
8								☺ ☹
9								☺ ☹
10								☺ ☹
11								☺ ☹
12								☺

APPENDIX B: TO DO LIST

To do list

	Mon	Tue	Wed	Thur	Fri
Week One					
Make bed	___	___	___	___	___
Put my stuff away	___	___	___	___	___
Finish homework	___	___	___	___	___
Week two	Mon	Tue	Wed	Thur	Fri
Make bed	___	___	___	___	___
Put my stuff away	___	___	___	___	___
Finish homework	___	___	___	___	___
Week three	Mon	Tue	Wed	Thur	Fri
Make bed	___	___	___	___	___
Put my stuff away	___	___	___	___	___
Finish homework	___	___	___	___	___
Week four	Mon	Tue	Wed	Thur	Fri
Make bed	___	___	___	___	___
Put my stuff away	___	___	___	___	___
Finish homework	___	___	___	___	___
Week five	Mon	Tue	Wed	Thur	Fri
Make bed	___	___	___	___	___
Put my stuff away	___	___	___	___	___
Finish homework	___	___	___	___	___
Week six	Mon	Tue	Wed	Thur	Fri
Make bed	___	___	___	___	___
Put my stuff away	___	___	___	___	___
Finish homework	___	___	___	___	___
Week seven	Mon	Tue	Wed	Thur	Fri
Make bed	___	___	___	___	___
Put my stuff away	___	___	___	___	___
Finish homework	___	___	___	___	___
Week eight	Mon	Tue	Wed	Thur	Fri
Make bed	___	___	___	___	___
Put my stuff away	___	___	___	___	___
Finish homework	___	___	___	___	___
Week nine	Mon	Tue	Wed	Thur	Fri
Make bed	___	___	___	___	___
Put my stuff away	___	___	___	___	___
Finish homework	___	___	___	___	___
Week ten	Mon	Tue	Wed	Thur	Fri
Make bed	___	___	___	___	___
Put my stuff away	___	___	___	___	___
Finish homework	___	___	___	___	___
Week eleven	Mon	Tue	Wed	Thur	Fri
Make bed	___	___	___	___	___
Put my stuff away	___	___	___	___	___
Finish homework	___	___	___	___	___

APPENDIX C: ACTION PLAN

White Belt Action Plan

Student Pledge:
    When:_____ Completed: Yes No
Terms: Chario, June bee, Kyunyee,
    When:_____ Completed: Yes No
Courtesies: Bow when entering and leaving room, say "Sir" to instructor, sit with feet folded, raise hand to ask question.
    When:_____ Completed: Yes No

(First eight lessons plus home practice)
Balance Kicks: Three count front kick,
    When: __8-15_____ Completed: Yes No
Basics: Reverse punch, back fist, stomach punch, front kick, Lurch step
    When: __8-22_____ Completed: Yes No

(Second eight plus home practice)
Blocks & Counters: Lounge punch, rising block, middle block, down block, front stance, horse stance, back stance.
    When: _____ Completed: Yes No
Pattern: WCRB Pattern # 1
    When: _____ Completed: Yes No

(Third eight lessons plus home practice)
Level one & two sparring: Target and rhythm
    When: _____ Completed: Yes No

Instructor's initials:
1st ___ __ ___ ___ ___ ___ ___ ___ **Test Date_8-27_** Balance & Basics
2nd ___ ___ ___ ___ ___ ___ ___ ___ **Test Date_9-24_** B&C & Pattern
3rd ___ ___ ___ ___ ___ ___ ___ ___ **Test Date_10-22_** Sparring
Report Card: ___1^{st}___2^{nd}___3^{RD}____final

How the Action Plan Works

At WCRB Karate, we are a goals oriented martial arts course. Here is how we introduce "School age" kids to the concept. After introducing them to the five necessary elements to obtain a goal: Realistic, Important, Yours, Action Plan and Time frame we next get them familiar with their "class card" Working with the "White belt Class Card", let's assume that a student signed up on Aug 1st 2018. Here is how a recommended "Action Plan" would work!

Assuming the child is coming two times a week, on Mondays and Wednesday. His start date would be Wednesday Aug 1st. His first "stripe test" would be on Aug 27th. In order to get his 1st stripe he would have to do: Balance Kick and Basics. In order to challenge himself, he would put Aug 15th down as the day he would know the balance kick, and Aug 22nd as the day he would know the basics. Note: that both dates have to be before the test date of the 27th. These dates are designed to give the process urgency!

His second stripe test would be on Sept 24th. In order to get his 2nd stripe he would have to do: Blocks and counters and the traditional pattern Chongi. In order to challenge himelf, he would put Sept 12th down as the day he would know the blocks and counters and the 19th as the day he will know the pattern. Again the date has to fit within the test date. Note: he does not have to wait until he knows the balance kick and basics to start working on the pattern. In fact in our classes it is recommended that he start working on the pattern as soon as possible.

His last test would be for his "Gold Belt" on the 22nd of October. He would put down a date of October 15th as the date that he will have his sparring good enough to be tested on.

Note also that, although the class "class card" "Action Plan" is filled out over 24 classes, the statement on the lower right of the card states that they have 48 practices sessions. This takes into consideration that the kids should practice two times a week at home.

At the end of the card it asked three important question: Is the goal realistic?, Is it something that THEY want to do?, and is it important?

Finally, the child is asked to sign the card to make the entire endeavor real.

Below please find a goals worksheet that can be used at home

Goal:
_____

Time Frame:
_____

Action Plan:
_____

Is this goal realistic? (Circle One)   Yes   No
Is this goal yours? (Circle One)   Yes   No
Is this goal important? (Circle One)   Yes   No
On a scale of 1-10 (ten being the highest) circle how important goal is:
1   2   3   4   5   6   7   8   9   10
Why is this goal important?
_____

Check Points		
Week One: On target	Yes	No
Week Two: On target	Yes	No
Week Three: On target	Yes	No
Week Four: On Target	Yes	No

APPENDIX D: About the Author, World Champion Rod Batiste

Rodney "Batman" Batiste is an 8th degree black belt, and has held the USA and World Middleweight Championship titles of the Professional Karate Association and the National Karate Association respectively.

Master Batiste has over 40 years of teaching experience, and is the recipient of several teaching and community service awards.

"Bat" has trained hundreds of black belts, as well as some notable celebrities, including AOL CEO emeritus James V. Kimsey, Congresswomen Jane Harman (former U.S. representative for California's 36 congressional district), Sidney Harman of Harman enterprises, Mary Wells of the Supremes, Richard Trumka (President of the AFL-CIO) and Warren Teitelbaum CEO of Mattress Discounters.

In the early 80's, when Master Batiste first conceived his **DAGPAW** concept, it was so well received that he was contracted by then Mayor Marion Barry to tour Washington D.C. doing seminars and lectures as part of his roaming leaders program; Ivan Labray of the Capitols and Wes Unsel of the Bullets were also part of the program.

In 1985 Master Batiste founded WCRB On-site Karate, the DC Area's premier provider of On-site martial arts services. Because of his unique **DAGPAW** teaching method and skills, and his organization's scope and method of instruction, his organization is awarded a wide range of teaching contracts annually from local and nationally recognized childcare facilities.

Here is a small list of educational facilities that have used Master Batiste's **DAGPAW** teaching method:

Arlington VA Elementary Schools: Science Focus, Arlington Traditional, Glebe, Ashlawn, Tuckahoe, McKinley, Oakridge, Long Branch, Key, and Drew.

DC area childcare facilities: KinderCare, Minnieland, La Petite, Springfield Academy, Bluebird Academy of Alexandria, Sparkles and more!

DC area recreational facilities: Arlington Parks and Recreation, Alexandria Parks and Recreation, Manassas Parks and Recreation, Falls Church Parks and Recreation.

The **DAGPAW** system is suitable for children and adults alike and caters to a wide range of ages from 2 ½ and up!

Interview conducted by Myles Burke

APPENDIX E: Martial Arts Studios Licensed to Teach the DAGPAW^{sm} Curriculum

WCRB Karate, Arlington, VA
Master Rod Batiste

WCRB Karate, Manassas Park, VA
Master Geoff Thompson

Your Studio, Your Town
Contact us to use the curriculum in your school.

The DAGPAW^{sm} curriculum is a service mark of WCRB Karate.

www.ingramcontent.com/pod-product-compliance
Lightning Source LLC
LaVergne TN
LVHW051512070426
835507LV00022B/3064